# Grumman F6F Hellcat

Zbigniew Kolacha

## Introduction

The WW2 American fighter the Grumman F6F Hellcat earned the title of "ace maker". No wonder, as some 307 aces fought in this type of fighter. Out of the 13 types of fighter aircraft used by the US Armed Forces during the entire war, this was the highest number. The best USAAF fighter was the North American P-51 Mustang, used by 275 aces. This success can be attributed to two factors: the number of Hellcats in action and the ease of flying the type. Many pilots mentioned that they liked flying this plane because it was pure pleasure. From the second half of 1943, the Hellcat entered service with all CV squadrons embarked on *Essex* – and *Independence*-class strike carriers (including CV-3 *Saratoga* and CV-6 *Enterprise*) as well as on escort carriers. The US Navy squadrons also operated from land bases located on various Pacific islands. In addition the F6F equipped several US Marine Squadrons. The only other user of the Hellcat outside the US during WW2 was the British Fleet Air Arm. The Hellcat saw action in all US Navy campaigns up to the last day of the war. It was a versatile aircraft. The great fighter worked very well as an attack aircraft, as well as an escort fighter for bombers and torpedo planes and as an air superiority interceptor.

The angular Hellcat was a masterpiece of engineering with a rugged design, with a powerful engine and powerful armament. In addition, it was easy to maintain, which is a very important feature of a carrier-borne aircraft. Despite the production of almost 12,000 aircraft, it did not undergo any major modifications because they were not needed. It performed perfectly in the role for which the engineers from Long Island designed it until the last day of WW2. The appearance of the Hellcat over the waters of the Pacific quickly tipped the scales of the war in favour of the Americans.

The Hellcat was much less manoeuvrable than most Japanese fighters, but its powerful engine allowed it to climb much faster than Japanese fighters, and it was also much faster in a dive. These two features gave Hellcat pilots a significant advantage. The "Thatch Weave" tactics developed for the earlier F4F Wildcat were used until the end of the war. Hellcat pilots used it even more effectively. In 1945, Gene Valencia improved the tactic by doubling the mutual insurance of pilots for the entire 4-plane section, consisting of two pairs, leading and wingman, the so-called. "division" (the USAAF equivalent was the same formation called a "flight"). The improved tactic was called "Valencia's lawnmower". All pilots flying in the Valencia section became aces.

In 1943, the nominal strength of a VF squadron was 36 machines on an *Essex*-class carrier and 24 on the Independence-class carriers. During the war, the US Navy Command made it a priority to keep the aircraft carriers afloat, especially after the successful kamikaze attacks near Leyte. Hence the number of fighter (Fighting) shipboard squadrons increased in 1945 to 74. CV-15 *Randolph* had as many F6Fs on board in May 1945 (there were no Corsairs on board the *Randolph*) divided for logistical reasons into VF and VBF, 34 each. In addition there were 4 night-fighter F6F-5Ns and 2 reconnaissance F6F-5Ps. From the beginning of 1945, after dealing with the logistical problems that had occurred earlier, squadrons flying the F4U Corsair, including squadrons of Marines, were embarked on the decks of aircraft carriers, as well as Hellcats. Corsairs, however, did not displace the Hellcats completely.

U.S. Navy and Marine Corps Hellcat pilots claimed a total of 5,156 kills of Japanese aircraft. This includes victories achieved at night and those achieved with the reconnaissance versions, F6F-3P and 5P. The British Hellcats in the Pacific added their own 47 victories. In Europe, Hellcats also shot down 13 German aircraft. The total number of aerial victories achieved by Hellcat pilots is therefore 5,216. Unfortunately, these successes were paid for by relatively high losses: 270 pilots died in combat, including 20 aces. Around 180 pilots were killed by air defences – a total of 450. The ratio of Hellcat victories to losses in aerial combat was still impressive at 19:1. A great result for an aircraft initially selected by the US Navy command as an interim aircraft, the successor to the weaker Wildcat. It was to take over the brunt of the fighting until the F4U Corsair, with better performance, was finalized, but work on the latter's improvement dragged on.

The most successful US Navy squadron was VF-15 with 310 victories. This unit operated from the aircraft carrier CV-9 *Essex*. Next were VF-9 (250.75) on *Essex*, *Lexington*, *Yorktown*, VF-2 (248) from *Enterprise & Hornet*), VF-18 (176.5) from *Intrepid*), VF-31 (165.6) from *Cabot & Belleau Wood*, VF-17 (161) from *Hornet*), VF-30 (159.83) from *Belleau Wood & Monterey*, VF-80 (159.5) from *Ticonderoga & Hancock*), VF-20 (158.16) from *Enterprise & Lexington*), VF-8-156 from Bunker Hill, etc.

Top U.S. Navy Ace was Cdr David McCampbell with 34 kills (all in the F6F), two-time ace in one day, and fourth on the list of all-time U.S. aces behind Richard Bong (40), Thomas McGuire (38) and Francis Gabreski 34.5 (28 WW2 + 6.5 Korean War). The second best Navy ace was Lt. Eugene Valencia with 24 kills, 6 in one day. Then Lt. Cecil Harris, also 24 (including 1 on F4F), Lt. Patrick Fleming, 19 including 5 in one day, Lt. Cornelius Noy, 19 including 5 in one day. All Noy's victories came in only 5 dogfights. Lt. Alexander Vraciu had 19, including 6 in one day.

The number of victories are according to the American Fighter Aces Association. Many victories were verified years after the war, usually increased.

Hellcat camouflage and markings will be described in part 2.

All of the Hellcat colour profiles in this book have been meticulously compiled from an extensive photo archive, numerous books, and much other source material.

1

**Grumman F6F-3 Hellcat, white 20 of VF-9 squadron.**

This aircraft based on the USS *Essex* (CV-9) aircraft carrier in May 1943.

The aircraft is wearing the standard camouflage pattern of NS Blue Gray over NS Light Gray.

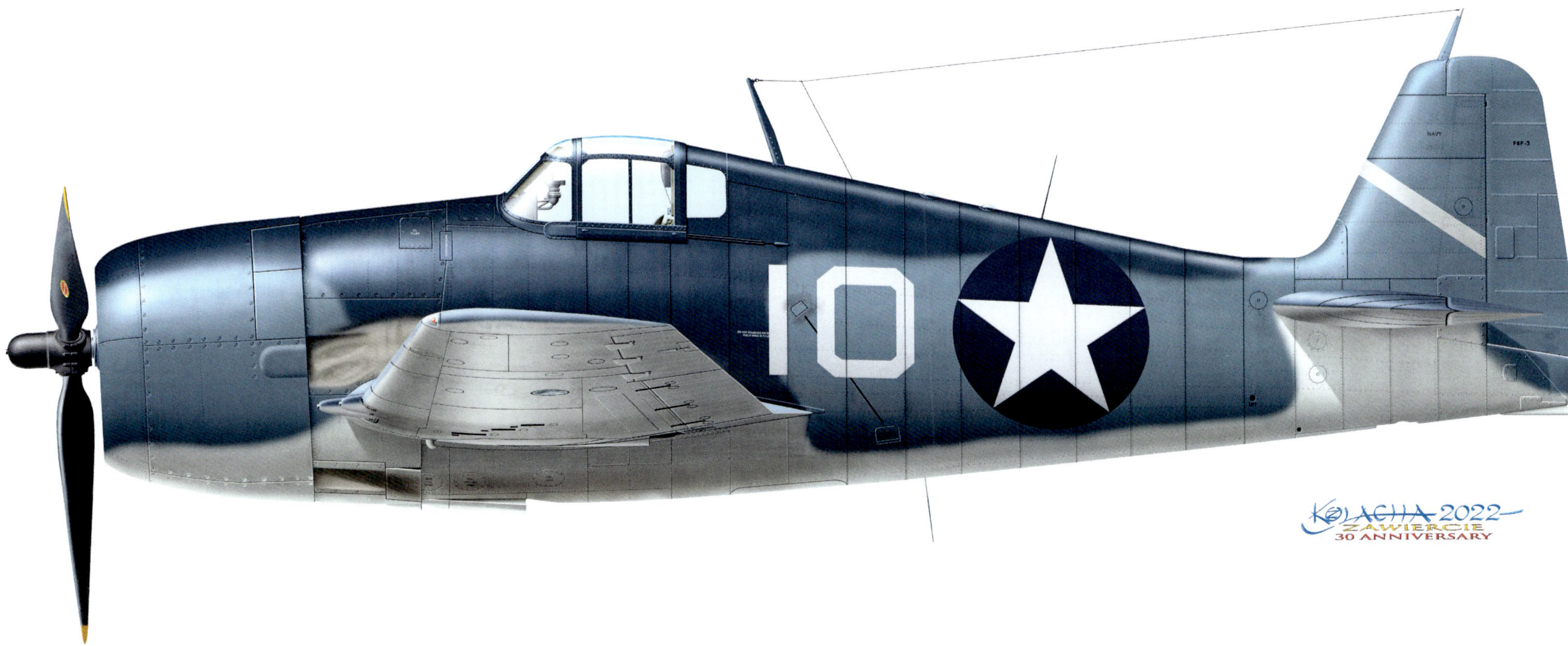


## Grumman F6F-3 Hellcat, white 10 of VF-10 squadron.

This aircraft based on the USS *Yorktown* (CV-10) aircraft carrier in May 1943.

The diagonal white stripe on the vertical stabilizer is the marking of the air group based on this carrier.

The aircraft is wearing the standard camouflage pattern of Non Specular Sea Blue, Intermediate Blue over White.

3

## Grumman F6F-3 Hellcat, white 10 of VF-10 squadron.

This aircraft based on the USS *Yorktown* (CV-10) aircraft carrier in early July 1943.

Red trim of national markings were introduced on June 26, 1943. This change was met with opposition due to the reintroduction of red into the national markings. The crew of the aircraft carrier *Yorktown* initially decided to reduce the size of the markings to make red less visible. It seems, however, that the repainting process was not completed because earlier Adm. Halsey issued a 300224 directive of July 31, 1943 ordering the removal of red borders for all aircraft of the SWPA theatre.

The aircraft is wearing the standard camouflage pattern of Non Specular Sea Blue, Intermediate Blue over White.

## Grumman F6F-3 Hellcat, white 00 of VF-10 squadron.

This aircraft based on the USS *Yorktown* (CV-10) aircraft carrier in early August 1943.

It is a personal aircraft of the commander of the CVG-10 Lt. Cdr. James H. Flatley. Factory-painted national markings were initially reduced with a red border. Later, red colour was painted over with Insignia Blue. Green on the spinner of the aircraft was the second marking of the aircraft carrier *Yorktown* until the last day of the war beyond the diagonal white stripe on the vertical stabilizer.

The aircraft is wearing the standard camouflage pattern of Non Specular Sea Blue, Intermediate Blue over White.

5

## Grumman F6F-3 Hellcat, white 61 of VF-12 squadron.

This aircraft based on the USS *Saratoga* (CV-3) aircraft carrier in early July 1943.

It is the personal aircraft of the commander of VF-12 Cdr. Joe C. Clifton. Aircraft captured in photographs during the change of orders with national markings. At that time, only white stripes were painted on the fuselage and the upper surface of the left wing. On the underside of the wings remained national insignia painted according to the previous rules. The aircraft is wearing the standard camouflage pattern of Non Specular Sea Blue, Intermediate Blue over White.

Grumman F6F-3 Hellcat,
white 61 of VF-12 squadron.

## Grumman F6F-3 Hellcat, white 12 of VF-15 squadron.

This aircraft based on the USS *Essex* (CV-9) aircraft carrier in October 1943.

This Hellcat bears clear signs of repainting camouflages and national markings.

The aircraft is wearing the standard camouflage pattern of Non Specular Sea Blue, Intermediate Blue over White.

Grumman F6F-3 Hellcat,
white 12 of VF-15 squadron.

9

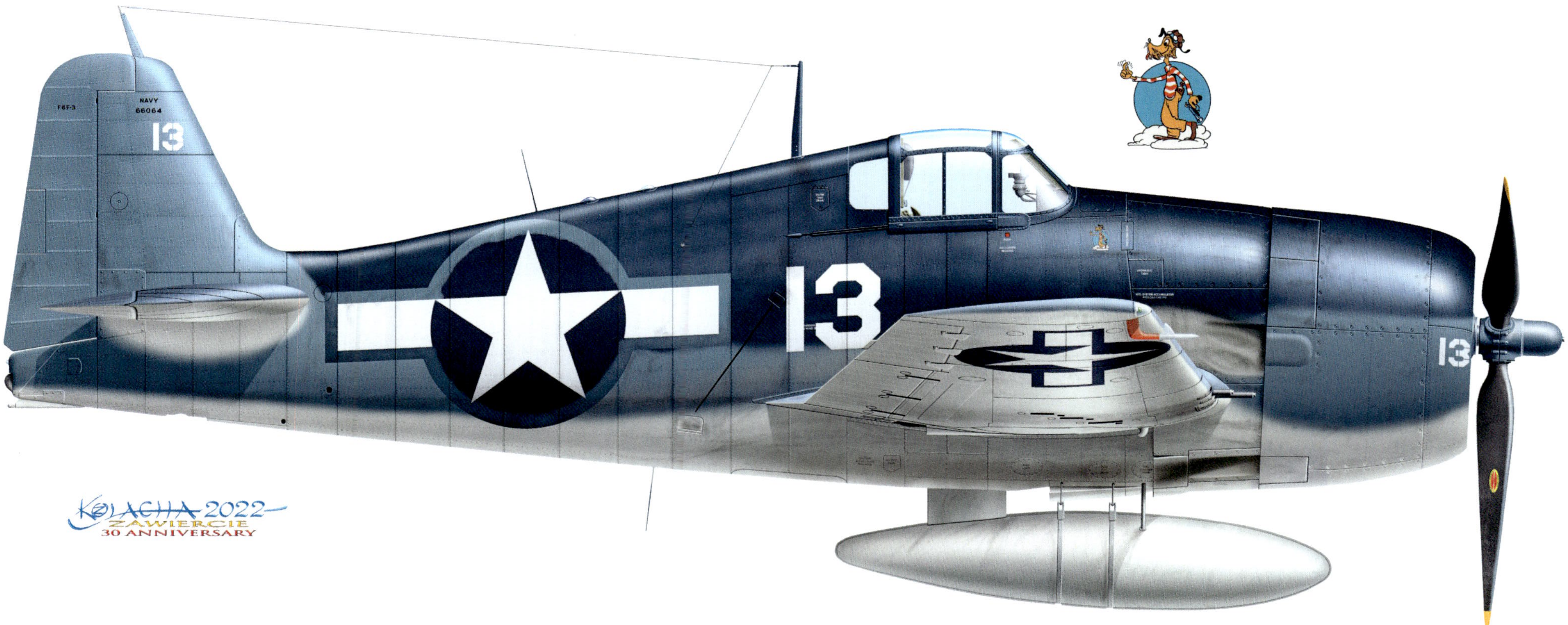


## Grumman F6F-3 Hellcat, BuNo 66064, white 13 of VF-16 squadron.

This aircraft based on the USS *Lexington* (CV-16) aircraft carrier in early December 1943.

Pilot – Ens. Edward O. Wendorf. The national isignias were modified by (carelessly) painting over the red trim with a mixture of Sea Blue, Intermediate Blue as a result of Adm. Halsey's No. 300224. On the underside of the right wing, the trim was painted over in Insignia Blue.

The aircraft is wearing the standard camouflage pattern of Non Specular Sea Blue, Intermediate Blue over White.

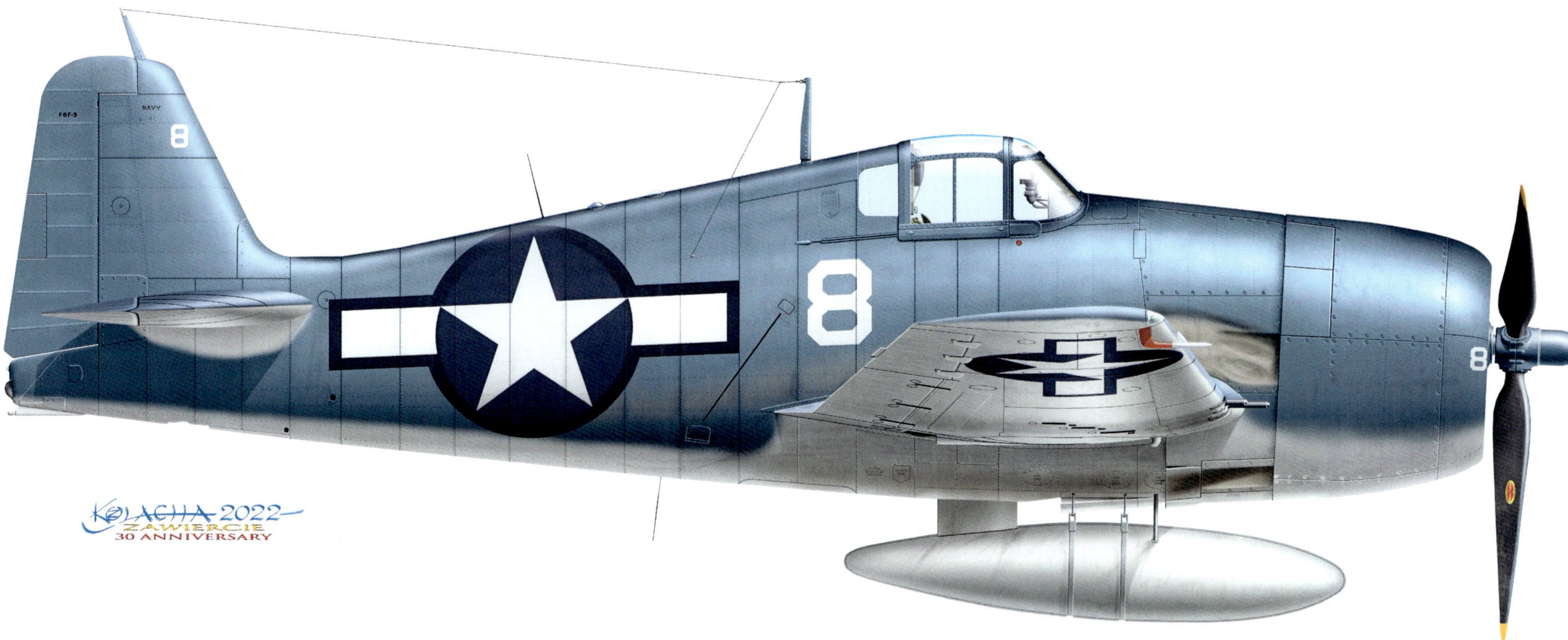


## Grumman F6F-3 Hellcat, white 8 of VF-16 squadron.

This aircraft based on the USS *Lexington* (CV-16) aircraft carrier in early February 1944.

Camouflage modified to renew the paint coating damaged as a result of many months of operation in the marine environment. Non Specular Sea Blue – wings, stabilizers and remnants of the upper surface of the fuselage, Intermediate Blue – sides of the fuselage and White – all lower surfaces.

11

## Grumman F6F-3 Hellcat, white 17 of VF-9 squadron.

This aircraft based on the USS *Essex* (CV-9) aircraft carrier in January 1944.

The aircraft wears large modifications of the factory camouflage resulting from replenishing paint wear and painting over the previous fuselage number. The national insignia have been modified by painting over the red trims with a mixture of Sea Blue and Intermediate Blue.

The aircraft is wearing the standard camouflage pattern of Non Specular Sea Blue, Intermediate Blue over White.

## Grumman F6F-3 Hellcat, white 24 of VF-9 squadron.

This aircraft based on the USS *Essex* (CV-9) aircraft carrier in February 1944.

Pilot – Lt. (jg) Gene Valencia – third on the list of aces of the US Navy, scored a total of 23 aerial victories. The aircraft bears large modifications of the factory camouflage resulting from replenishing the deteriorating paint coating and painting over the previous fuselage number. The national markings have been modified by painting over the red trims with a mixture of Sea Blue and Intermediate Blue.

The aircraft is wearing the standard camouflage pattern of Non Specular Sea Blue, Intermediate Blue over White.

13

## Grumman F6F-3 Hellcat, white 21 of VF-8 squadron.

This aircraft based on the USS *Bunker Hill* (CV-17) aircraft carrier in July 1944.

The aircraft wears modifications of the factory camouflage resulting from the replenishment of the deteriorating paint coating. Below and above the tactical number, the 2 white lines visible were the markings of USS *Bunker Hill* based aircraft until January 1945.

The aircraft is wearing the standard camouflage pattern of Non Specular Sea Blue, Intermediate Blue over White.

## Grumman F6F-3 Hellcat, white 26 of VF-2 squadron.

This aircraft based on the USS *Hornet* (CV-12) aircraft carrier in April 1944.

Below tactical number 26, a visible white circle was the marking of USS *Hornet* based aircraft until January 1945.

The aircraft is wearing the standard camouflage pattern of Non Specular Sea Blue, Intermediate Blue over White.

15

## Grumman F6F-3 Hellcat, white 1 of VF-6 squadron.

This aircraft based on the USS *Interpid* (CV-11) aircraft carrier in February 1944.

It was a personal aircraft of (most likely) the commander of VF-6 Lt. Cdr H. W. Harrison. Below tactical number 1, a white line, was the markings of CVG-6 aircraft based on USS *Intrepid* in January and February 1944.

The aircraft is wearing the standard camouflage pattern of Non Specular Sea Blue, Intermediate Blue over White.

## Grumman F6F-3 Hellcat, white 19 “Gadget”, BuNo 40467 of VF-6 squadron.

This aircraft based on the USS *Interpid* (CV-11) aircraft carrier in February 1944.

Personal aircraft of Lt. (jg) Alexander Vraciu, an ace with 19 victories.

The aircraft is wearing the standard camouflage pattern of Non Specular Sea Blue, Intermediate Blue over White.

17

## Grumman F6F-3 Hellcat, white 11 of VF-1 squadron.

This aircraft based on the USS *Yorktown* (CV-10) aircraft carrier in July 1944.

The aircraft wears standard factory camouflage. The green nose was an additional identification mark for aircraft from the USS *Yorktown*, regardless of the currently embarked CVG air group, until the end of the war. A diagonal white stripe on the fin, was the primary identification of this carrier's aircraft until January 1945. The aircraft is wearing the standard camouflage pattern of Non Specular Sea Blue, Intermediate Blue over White.

Grumman F6F-3 Hellcat,
white 11 of VF-1 squadron.

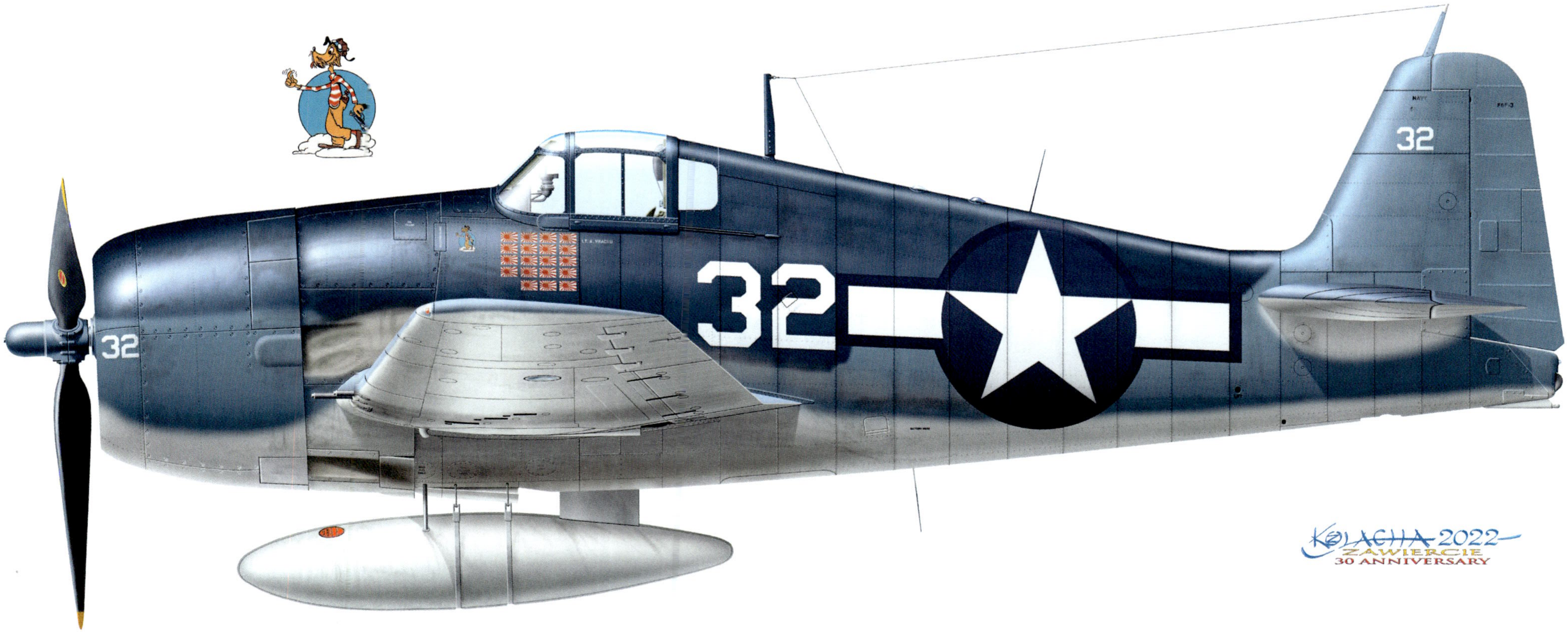


## Grumman F6F-3 Hellcat, white 32 of VF-16 squadron.

This aircraft based on the USS *Lexington* (CV-16) aircraft carrier in June 1944.
The pilot of this machine was Lt. Alexander Vraciu, ace with 19 victories. Previously, he was a VF-6 pilot embarked aboard the USS *Intrepid*.
The aircraft is wearing the standard camouflage pattern of Non Specular Sea Blue, Intermediate Blue over White.

## Grumman F6F-3 Hellcat, white 31 of VF-18 squadron.

This aircraft based on the USS *Interpid* (CV-11) aircraft carrier in October 1944.

The aircraft wears standard factory camouflage. The white cross on the fin was used as a sign of quick identification of aircraft from the USS *Intrepid* between August and November 1944, only by CVG-18.

The aircraft is wearing the standard camouflage pattern of Non Specular Sea Blue, Intermediate Blue over White.

21

## Grumman F6F-3P Hellcat, white 35 "Prophet" of VF-15 squadron.

This aircraft based on the USS *Essex* (CV-9) aircraft carrier in May 1944.

The pilot of this machine was Lt. Robert Paul Fash, an ace with 6 victories. This Hellcat wears standard factory camouflage. It is a reconnaissance version, equipped with 2 cameras – one on the right side of the hull for oblique photos and the other for vertical photos on the bottom of the fuselage. The white stripe on the fins was a sign of quick identification of USS *Essex* aircraft until January 1945.

The aircraft is wearing the standard camouflage pattern of Non Specular Sea Blue, Intermediate Blue over White.

## Grumman F6F-3 Hellcat, white 23 of VF-27 squadron.

This aircraft based on the USS *Princeton* (CVL-23) aircraft carrier in October 1944.

The pilot of this machine was Lt. James Alexander "Red" Shirley, an ace with 12.5 victories. This Hellcat wears standard factory camouflage. The mouth of a hell-cat with eyes became a sign of quick identification of the Hellcats of the USS *Princeton*.

The aircraft is wearing the standard camouflage pattern of Non Specular Sea Blue, Intermediate Blue over White.

23

## Grumman F6F-5 Hellcat, white 69, BuNo 58468 of VF-20 squadron.

This aircraft based on the USS *Enterprise* (CV-6) aircraft carrier in November 1944.

The white triangle on the fin is a sign of quick identification of USS *Enterprise* aircraft used until January 1945.

Aircraft Glossy Sea Blue overall.

## Grumman F6F-5 Hellcat, "Minsi III", BuNo 70143 of CVG-15.

This aircraft based on the USS *Essex* (CV-9) aircraft carrier in October 1944.

Personal aircraft of Cdr David McCampbell, CVG-15 commander. The most famous and popularized Hellcat imaginable, as David McCampbell was the first on the list of US Navy aces – 34 aerial victories – and until the end of the war no one beat his score. The absence of any side number in this case, is marking of the commander of Air Group 15. Small CAG letters on the fin and on the undercarriage covers are an abbreviation for Commander Air Group. Aircraft Glossy Sea Blue overall.

25

**Grumman F6F-5 Hellcat, white 17, “Ripper”, BuNo 70328 of VF-7 squadron.**

This aircraft based on the USS *Hancock* (CV-19) aircraft carrier in October 1944.

Aircraft Glossy Sea Blue overall.

## Grumman F6F-5 Hellcat, white 10, BuNo 70574 of VF-15 squadron.

This aircraft based on the USS *Essex* (CV-19) aircraft carrier in October 1944.

Personal aircraft of Lt. Cdr George Chamberlain Duncan, an ace with 13.5 victories.

Aircraft Glossy Sea Blue overall.

27

## Grumman F6F-5N Hellcat, white 21 of VFN-20.

This aircraft based on the USS *Enterprise* (CV-6) aircraft carrier in February 1945.

The white horizontal arrow on the vertical stabilizer is a quick identification mark (G-Symbol) for aircraft carriers *Enterprise* since January 1945. Wings without this sign. The white spinner is an informal designation for the Hellcats from the aircraft carrier *Enterprise*.

Aircraft Glossy Sea Blue overall.

## Grumman F6F-5 Hellcat, white 59 of VF-53 squadron.

This aircraft based on the USS *Saratoga* (CV-3) aircraft carrier in February 1945.

The white chevron on the fin, and the same mark on the upper surface of the right wing, is a sign of quick identification of aircraft carriers *Saratoga* from January 1945. The green and white spinner is the informal designation of the *Saratoga* Hellcats.

Aircraft Glossy Sea Blue overall.

29

Grumman F6F-5 Hellcat, white 59
of VF-53 squadron.

## Grumman F6F-5 Hellcat, white 19 of VF-9 squadron.

This aircraft based on the USS *Lexington* (CV-16) aircraft carrier in March 1945.

Pilot unknown. White diagonal stripe on the fin and only on the upper surfaces of both wings. It is a sign of the rapid identification of the aircraft based at *Lexington* from January to July 1945. Aircraft Glossy Sea Blue overall.

31

## Grumman F6F-5 Hellcat, white 31 of VF-17squadron.

This aircraft based on the USS *Hornet* (CV-12) aircraft carrier in April 1945.

The white checkerboard on the fin, and on the upper surfaces of both wings, is a sign of quick identification of the aircraft based at USS *Hornet* since January 1945. The white nose is the identification mark of aircraft, which was introduced before the attack of TF 58 on the island of Kyushu on 18 and 19 March 1945. Operation of the destruction of Japanese airfields, as a preparation for the landing on Okinawa. It is not known when markings were deleted, but it seems that it were still used in the first days of Operation Iceberg – the landing of Okinawa on April 1, 1945. Aircraft Glossy Sea Blue overall.

## Grumman F6F-5P Hellcat, white 69 of VF-85 squadron.

This aircraft based on the USS *Shangri-La* (CV-38) aircraft carrier in June 1945.

White lightning on the stabilizer and on the upper surfaces of the right and lower left wings is a sign of quick identification of *Shangri-La* aircraft from January to July 1945. In August 1945, the "G-symbol" was replaced by letter designations. USS *Shangri-La* was given a letter code – Z. The previous signs were painted over, and the letter Z appeared on the flight deck in place of number 38. In 1945, on board this carrier there were 2 Hellcats in the reconnaissance version with numbers 68 and 69. Aircraft Glossy Sea Blue overall.

## Grumman F6F-3 Hellcat, black 100 of VF-38 squadron.

This aircraft based at Munda land base, New Georgia. June 1944.

Most likely, it is the plane of the squadron commander. White paint elements indicate a friendly plane. The squadron operated from land airfields and cooperated with USAAF and US units Marines, as well as RAAF and RNZAF. U.S. Navy squadrons were not subject to Army Command Technical Orders where the tails of fighter aircraft were painted white, but VF-38 personnel decided to wear a similar livery for safety.

The aircraft is wearing the standard camouflage pattern of Non Specular Sea Blue, Intermediate Blue over White.

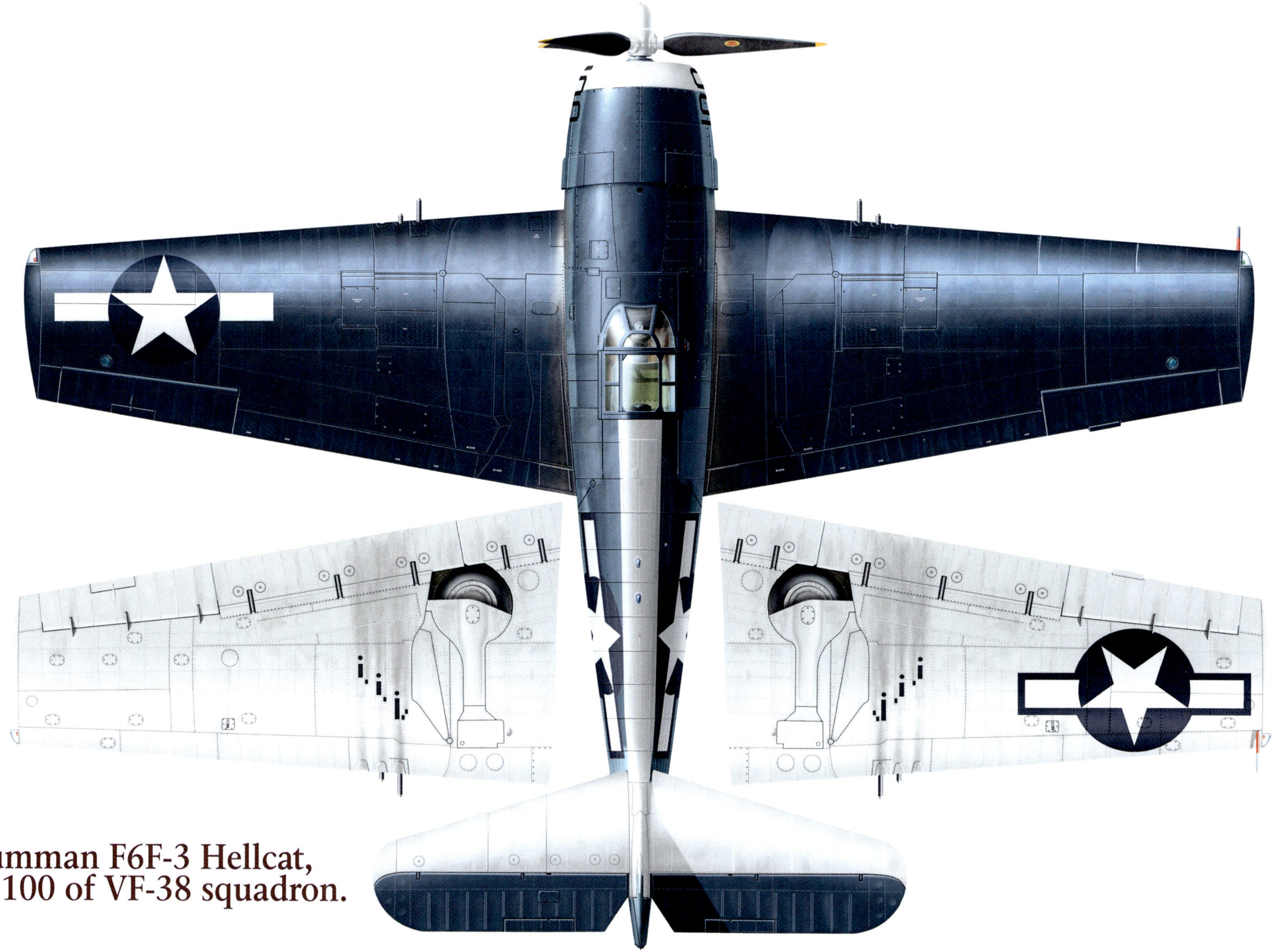

Grumman F6F-3 Hellcat, black 100 of VF-38 squadron.

## Hellcat Mk I, JV108, E*B of 800 FAA squadron.

Hellcat Mk I, JV108 E*B of No. 800 Squadron FAA from the aircraft carrier HMS *Emperor* (D98). Aegean Sea, September 1944.

Camouflage: Extra Dark Sea Grey, Dark Slate Grey, Sky.

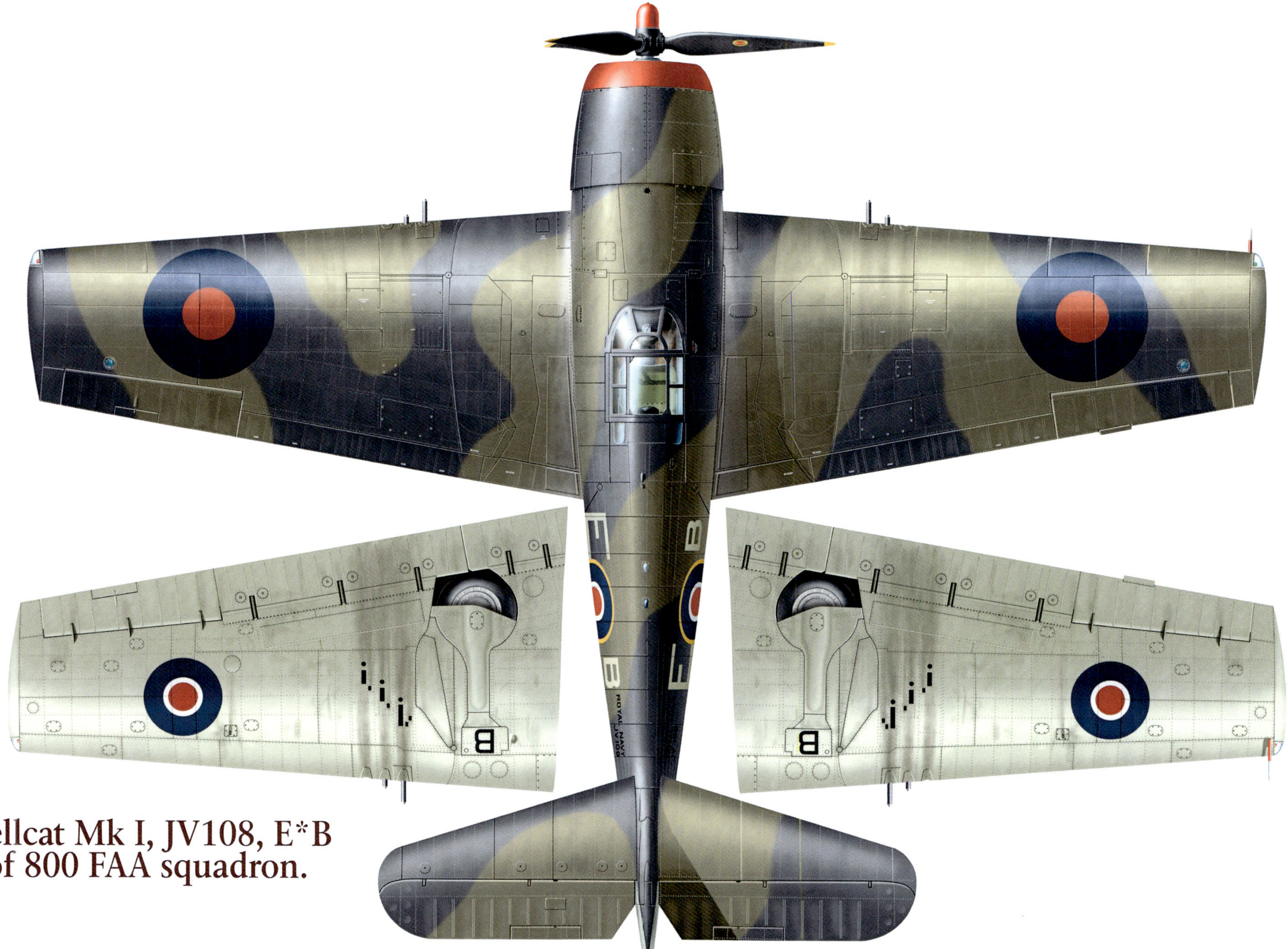


Hellcat Mk I, JV108, E*B
of 800 FAA squadron.

Published in Poland in 2023
by STRATUS sp.j.
Po. Box 123,
27-600 Sandomierz 1, Poland
e-mail: office@mmpbooks.biz
as
MMPBooks,

e-mail: office@mmpbooks.biz



**ISBN**
978-83-67227-04-9

*Editor in chief*
Roger Wallsgrove

*Editorial Team*
Bartłomiej Belcarz
Robert Pęczkowski
Artur Juszczak

*Colour profiles*
Zbigniew Kolacha

*DTP*
Stratus sp.j.

*Printed by*
Wydawnictwo Diecezjalne i Drukarnia w Sandomierzu
www.wds.pl

PRINTED IN POLAND

# Also in this series.

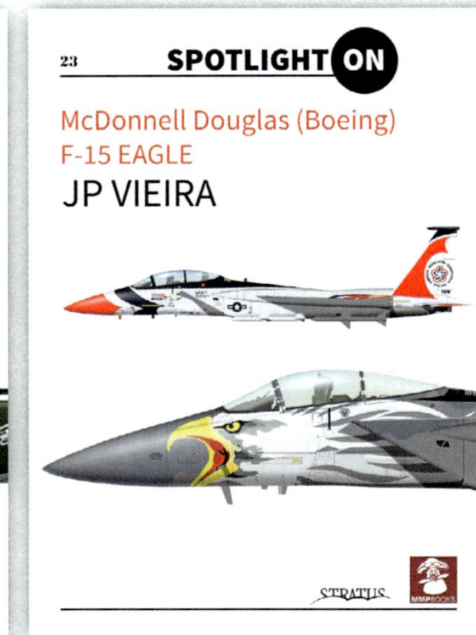


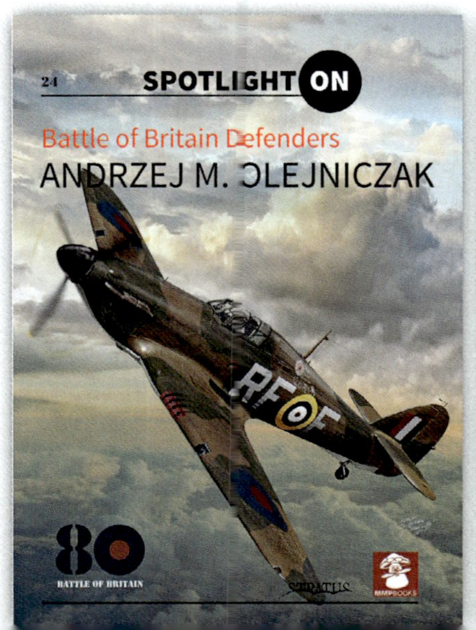